PRAISE FOR *NOW WHAT?* *MANAGING A SUDDEN* *TRANSITION IN YOUR CAREER*

Now What? Managing a Sudden Transition in your Career is a great read for those who have been in the unenviable position of no position. Annella Metoyer candidly extracts the fears, anguish, and vulnerabilities associated with what can be described as one of life's underestimated tragedies. At the same time, she does a great job illustrating healing and hope with real-life examples to which we can all relate. *Now What?* is a must-read, especially for those who seek peace and an answer.

—Ray Pereira, Regional Bank Executive

Through her own personal recount and those provided by others that have experienced a similar fate, Ms. Metoyer captures the essence of what it truly feels like to be displaced.

—Cynthia Calapa Riezenman, **former banking colleague**

Now What? should be required reading for anyone who believes that saying "it's a business decision—it isn't personal" is helpful or respectful when informing someone that they are being laid off. The importance of work in our lives cannot be overstated. In addition to financial security, it is central to our relationships, a sense of purpose and value, and identity. In *Now What?* Annella offers readers a glimpse into the gut-wrenching, life-changing experience of what it is like to lose a job due to forces outside your control. The stories, including her own, provide a first-hand look at the aftermath of the often sterile and abrupt end to years of dedication and contribution: the shock, disorientation, doubt, and many other emotions. For anyone who is or has been "in transition," many of the experiences will probably be familiar.

The book also offers hope and inspiration for anyone at any stage of the transition process. For those stumbling disoriented through a tunnel of doubt, the stories of those who have crawled and clawed their way to the other side can help put things in perspective; falling and getting up is part of the process. For those who don't know where to start, Annella shares practical tips, suggestions, and small steps to move forward, including the importance of reaching out for help. For those looking for answers about what to do in the next phase of their lives, her message is clear: as awful as this experience may seem, it can be a wake-up call. Reflect, learn, and move forward with confidence with your eyes wide open.

Losing a job is always disruptive, and the chaos of the current environment adds an extra level of pressure to an already overwhelming experience. While there are no easy answers, this book offers nuggets of wisdom from the generous heart of someone who has traveled the path and is dedicated to helping and serving others on the journey.

—**Angela Stauder, Managing Director, Personalysis**

Now What?

Managing a Sudden Transition in Your Career

By

Annella Metoyer

Book cover photo by Michael Metoyer
Editing by Eye Comb Editors (www.eyecombeditors.com)
Book cover design and interior design by JetLaunch, LLC
(www.jetlaunch.net)
Illustrations by Gaby Sennes and Rinesh Bajracharya

Annella Metoyer books are available for order through Amazon.com.
Visit my website: www.annellametoyer.com
Twitter: @MetoyerAnnella
Facebook: www.facebook.com/annellametoyer
LinkedIn: www.linkedin.com/in/annellametoyer
Instagram: www.instagram.com/annellametoyer/

Printed in the United States of America
First Printing: June 2021
Published by Inspire Development, LLC.

ISBN-13: [978-1-64184-198-6] (Hardback)
ISBN-13: [978-1-64184-199-3] (paper)
ISBN-13: [978-1-64184-200-6] (Kindle)

Disclaimer:
The contents of this book is for informational purposes only and is not a substitute for professional medical or legal advice. If you choose to rely on any information provided in *Now What? Managing a Sudden Transition in Your Career,* you do so solely at your own risk. Under no circumstances is the author or Inspire Development, LLC responsible for the claims of third-party websites or educational providers.

Some names and identifying details have been changed to protect the privacy of the individuals.

DEDICATION

This handbook is dedicated to the many individuals who have experienced a transition, termination, reduction in force, separation, or displacement in the workplace.

Courage is the power to let go of the familiar

—Raymond Lindquist

TABLE OF CONTENTS

FOREWORD

If you've transitioned out of a job, then you have probably heard one or more attempts to cheer you up. Such attempts probably didn't work.

"It's just a job."

It's just a place you go to Monday through Friday. You live there for forty to sixty hours a week. You work hard to do a good job, make a difference, and prove yourself. However, it becomes who you are. When asked to describe yourself, your first answer is, "I'm a banker," or whatever your job or title is at the time.

"They aren't your friends. They are just co-workers."

They are just co-workers who know your kids' names and your favorite lunch spot. You have spent late nights together working and collaborating on countless projects. You depend on and appreciate them as people, not just faces in the office. They are supportive in good and challenging times . . . yet where are they now?

I told Annella, "It's their loss. Now you get to enjoy your free time," when she told me she was leaving her company. She and Michael were in town, and we met for lunch. She told me she had decided to leave her position at the bank. I was happy for her because she was the hardest working person I knew. Annella's efforts had gained her respect and accolades, and I thought she was retiring at the top of her game. Good for her! I never considered she wasn't leaving on her own. It took me a second to realize she wasn't smiling or happy. She was sad. I tried to be positive, although there wasn't anything to say that would heal the pain she was feeling.

Annella and I had first met at work. She had been my boss, and I, her secretary. She was the first supervisor I'd ever had who would introduce me as working "alongside" her rather than working "for" her. She was sharp and professional. She was a dedicated and loyal employee of every company, past and present. She taught me structure and excellence, and her living example influenced those around her. She was who you wanted to represent your company and to lead your team. It's been over twenty years since we met, and I admire and respect her as my mentor and friend more than ever.

In this book, Annella does what she does best. She's lifting others and giving them hope and strength by sharing her knowledge and lived experience. Annella tells her story and those of others who have dealt with transitions from their jobs. She describes the different stages she experienced while healing and moving to a new phase of her life. Through the telling of others' stories, she illustrates that, while they each experienced the end of their job, it was not the final chapter in their life.

NOW WHAT?

If you have experienced the loss of a job and you are wondering, *Now what?* read this book. Let Annella's words give you hope that you can move on and that you are not alone. Loss is hard, but hope endures.

—Denise C. LeBlanc, Chief Financial Officer of Spindletop Center and Author of *He Was*

PREFACE

When the president of the bank I worked at decided to transition out of banking, her final parting words to me were, "Know when it's time to step away." Less than five years after she spoke those words, I found myself at a crossroads. I had worked over forty years in banking, fully expecting to retire at a much later date, possibly as late as seventy years old. However, at fifty-nine years old, I faced a career-changing decision. Banking was changing rapidly; the digital age continued to reduce the need for bank offices and associates. With fewer offices, territories were consolidated, requiring fewer executives in retail. After each meeting, my peers and I would ask ourselves, *Who will be the next person laid off?*

You realize it's your turn when your boss talks to you about considering another position inside the company. *Another department? Are you telling me I am next?* I was next and not ready to leave the company. With a smile on my face and my heart broken, I took a leap of faith and recreated my career.

This handbook shares my journey of a sudden career change, the stories of others, and the lessons we learned about ourselves.

—Annella Metoyer

ACKNOWLEDGMENTS

I want to thank all the individuals who shared their stories. Also, thank you to the past associates—too many to name—I have worked alongside throughout my career. You have given me many gifts of growth. I am a better person because of you, and I will continue to pay it forward by helping others.

I don't live to work; I work to live.

—Noel Gallagher

1

Transition, Termination, Reduction in Force, Separation, & Displacement

The terms "transition," "termination," "reduction in force," "separation," and "displacement" all have one thing in common: *fear*. Fear of the unknown, fear of change, or fear of an uncertain future. Many of my friends and colleagues shared their stories about the day they each broke up with their company. Some were aware in advance due to a reorganization of the company—like a buy-out or merger—while others were surprised by the bad news. Whether the displacement is a surprise, or you see the "writing on the wall," it's an exhausting process.

It was a beautiful warm morning, and I started my day like any other—coffee, breakfast, and NPR news—as I drove to my first meeting. Today was not like any other day because today the leadership team would undergo restructuring. For the first time since their reassignment four years prior, my boss and the human resources consultant visited my region and joined our annual regional leaders' offsite meeting. Together we reviewed the previous year's successes and opportunities and strategized for the new year. As I watched my boss and the human resources consultant take notes and talk to each other, I felt an uneasiness in my core. I had survived the first, second, and third reorganization of the company, yet today I would not survive this restructuring of the department.

After 2007, discussion focused on the iPhone, Facebook, and other social media tools. Because of the low cost of information traveling at warp speeds, we continued to see digital data replace paper, reducing the number of employees needed to do a job. The 2008 market downturn, we saw companies shifting focus to technology. In 2010, I also saw massive shifts in the leadership teams. The reorganizations eliminated positions held, in many cases, for over twenty years. I watched friends who had a wealth of knowledge and skills exit the company. I would lay sleepless wondering, *Did someone in the company capture their knowledge, or did the company no longer have a need for the information?* As when someone is dying, do we write down their life journey for others, or do we bury the chapters with them?

While driving to the meeting to debrief the conference with my boss, I knew my immediate future included a transition out of the company. As I trudged into the conference room, I prayed to find the right words. My boss sat across the table from me. The debrief started with her feedback about the conference. She continued by saying, "The company decided to lower the number of retail executives, and someone will lose their job."

When your boss talks about the displacement and does not assure you of your continued tenure in the company, you know the time has come to make other plans for your future. Fear clouded my mind. *Would I find another job? What would I tell my family? What will I say when I walk out of my office?* I waited for her to share my value to the company. Instead, she advised, "Consider other departments you can interview for. I can connect you with the right person for a new position." However, I did not want to work in another department; I loved my job and the people I had worked beside for many years. I desired only to hear my value to the company. Those words did not come.

Lots of conversing with my husband helped me realize the reality. He said, "Honey, if she wanted you to stay, she would have talked to you about your new responsibilities. Instead, she asked you to interview with another department. Can you continue to live in the unknown?"

I decided it was best to take the severance package. I could not continue working for someone who did not see my value. I felt defeated after years and years of survival. Now, I had to face my fear, tap into my power, and determine my next chapter.

*Any transition is easier if you
believe in yourself and your talent.*

—Priyanka Chopra

CHAPTER 2

STEPS THROUGH A TRANSITION

When a career transition happened to me, I stopped breathing. I stepped into denial. Reviewing and approving my severance package became a top priority, however my chest hurt like someone pressing on it when I tried to read the document. I resisted the reality of a final step away from the company.

Who am I? What will I stand for? When employed, I had no problem answering these questions. Now I questioned my self-worth and what to do next. Should I find another job, or should I step out and do something different? Losing my identity paralyzed me, and I continued to question why I lost my job. Did I not play politics correctly? Did I fail to recognize individuals who supported me in my absence by being my "voice in the room"? Did I fail to be flexible and open to my boss's expectations?

I told myself to rise above and not give in to the emotional fallout of transition. Nevertheless, I would barrel forward to my new venture. Despite my efforts,

I experienced all the phases of transition: shock, anger, joy, fear, guilt, depression, risk, recovery, and empowerment. Everyone's pilgrimage through transition is different, and the stages do not always occur in a specific order.

STEP 1: SHOCK

After an announcement of an organizational change, everyone has a different reaction. Some feel shocked, whie others feel surprised. Then come the questions: *Will the change affect me? Am I losing my job? Now, what?* After an announcement like this, workplace productivity declines. For many employees, work remains at a standstill, as they wonder, *How can I do my daily job when my future is uncertain, and the company has not answered my questions to my satisfaction?*

Steve's Story

After working over ten years at a large corporation, I traveled to the home office the week before Christmas for what I thought would be my annual performance review. When I arrived, my manager invited me to take a seat, and with no prior warning, my position was eliminated. Shocked and confused, I struggled with the company's decision to let me go. For the last four quarters, my team ranked number one. *Why choose me instead of someone else?* I remember feeling appalled by the sterile approach taken in eliminating my role. My manager never looked at me, only at the papers on the desk. Paralyzed by the news, I sat in a daze. Doubts about my skills flooded my mind. *Number one in the company, and I am being asked to leave? Why me? How will I tell my family? Will I be able to take care of my family?*

How do you cope despite the shock of an announcement potentially affecting your livelihood? News of my departure spread quickly. A coworker called me and said, "The universe has spoken; it's a blessing in disguise. You will have time to do what you were called to do." Shocked, I rejected seeing my job loss as a blessing. I knew my employer had made a mistake and would call me to come back to work. How could a mistake be a blessing?

Susan's Story

Everything changed in June 2016. I was only nine months into my new role and working on two initiatives for the company. I was putting the finishing touches on a presentation when my vice president passed by my desk and told me he needed to see me in his office.

He had just joined the company three months earlier, and because of his extensive travels, we had yet to meet one on one. Excited for some time to finally get to know him, I followed him to his office. On the way, I asked a few questions about his move to the area and whether he liked living here. He nodded yes although he did not expand on details. When we got to his office, he opened the door and motioned for me to come in.

As soon as I stepped through the door, I saw a member of human resources sitting at a conference table. Her eyes were moist and puffy, and she continued dabbing her nose with a tissue. Now I didn't need to be a detective to figure out what would happen next. I sat down, and my boss said, "Unfortunately for you, Susan, I have a brief announcement to make. As you know, we're taking a different approach to change management, and you're no longer qualified for the position, so we are eliminating your role effective today. Our decision to eliminate your position is not performance-based, so you have sixty days to find another role in the company." No "Thank you for your contributions." No "I appreciate your hard work." No "Our decision was hard, however it's what's best for the company." Instead, he walked toward the door, indicating the conversation was over while waving to the human resources representative to hurry up and go over my severance package.

Wow, I thought to myself, *He did not bother to get to know me or my qualifications. I wonder if he's seen my resume or recognizes all the major projects I have led. I wonder if he knows the company paid thousands of dollars to train and certify me in change management. I wonder if he knows my personal story.* A year earlier, I'd lost my youngest brother to cancer, and my work had provided me a source of happiness and stability.

The emotion I remember feeling: disappointment. Not because the company let me go—I understand how business works, and sometimes companies have to make tough decisions to help them operate more efficiently. I was disappointed my boss did not treat me as a human being but as a number. I am not any different from any other employee. I have a family to take care of, a career I love, and many financial obligations. Yet, on my final day of employment, I was just a name on a spreadsheet. For weeks, I waited for the company to call me back to my old job. I was hoping they would say "We are sorry; we made a mistake" or "We want you back."

You may have feelings of confusion, denial, ambivalence, or fear. Do not make choices at the shock stage. The best advice is to breathe deeply and spend time taking care of yourself.

ANGER

Step 2: Anger

Employees express anger if the path to their next opportunity is ambiguous. If questions are not clearly and quickly answered, employees may feel unsupported by management. One example of a question is: "Will I have a job?"

> *Amber's Story*
>
> My boss sent me an appointment request. At the meeting, she began listing the items she felt I did not perform to her satisfaction. She also shared that two vice presidents for the assigned client group no longer desired me to be their human resources liaison. I asked her for the reasons, yet she said she did not know. I also asked her what I could do to improve. She again answered she did not know what I should do differently. At the end of the meeting, she requested a plan of action to mitigate the problem. I started asking myself, *Is she attempting to eliminate my position?* Anger set in because I respected my boss, a person responsible for leading, supporting, and developing me. After the meeting, I took the weekend to replay the exchange. Instead of building up more anger, I decided to give my separation notice the following Monday. Moving forward became my choice, given the ambiguity of the situation.

Sometimes employees will select out of a job if they feel no support from management. Amber loved her job and knew if her supervisor didn't support her, she would not be successful.

In transition, acknowledge your emotions. To prevent an angry outburst, do not dwell on feeling underappreciated; instead, focus on the moments you felt appreciated. Assess what the change will mean for your future and how you can best manage it. Make a list of questions to ask your boss and consider seeking other opportunities within the company. If alternatives are not available within the company, seek options in your "power source": your network, coach, family, and other members of your circle.

STEP 3: JOY

On the other hand, sometimes employees have feelings of exhilaration when change occurs because the environment may have been one of hostility. Some will say, "Thank goodness," because the current culture does not meet their expectations. They feel joy in the transformation bringing new opportunities.

Gail's Story

I had worked for my company for over ten years. For the last three years, layoffs had continued every six months. My day came when a regular conference call turned into a severance notice. We had thirty days to wrap up our daily duties, pack our office, and say our goodbyes. Finally, no more sleepless nights, stomachaches, or headaches. At the end of the call, all I wanted to say was, "Give me my severance package and let me live again."

While one person may feel joy where another feels anger, the outcome is the same: they are no longer employed, inviting fear.

FEAR

STEP 4: FEAR

Fear is an emotional response to unknown and uncertain threats. When your company restructures your department, fear can trigger the real or imaginary threat of losing your income or livelihood.

No longer working for the company, a friend called to check on me. As we talked about my new chapter, she gave me some unsolicited advice. She said, "Until you take your toe out of the water, you will not move forward."

When I asked her to explain, she said, "You still identify with your previous job and title versus seeing yourself as a person working for a company." I paused, puzzled. "Who would I be if not a banker?"

Fear blurred my vision. Besides losing my identity as a banker after forty years, I felt concerned about my age. Would a company hire a fifty-nine-year-old? The loud noise played in my head, and I started doubting my skills and years of experience.

Are you fearful because you listen to the negative voice whispering in your ear? Are you fearful your skill level is subpar for your next opportunity? Instead of living in fear, focus on the bigger world that you can help, and make a difference in the lives of others.

STEP 5: GUILT

I experienced guilt during my transition because I felt I had abandoned my colleagues in accepting the severance package. I had always seen myself as a champion for the underdog, standing up for individuals who may not have found their voice among management. Now who would be the voice for them? What if I had interviewed for another position in the company? Maybe I would have adjusted quickly. Why had I not at least attempted?

I loved the company and the people I had worked alongside for many years. I remember sitting on the porch and feeling both overwhelmed and guilty.

Choices like accepting a severance package may affect your livelihood, so once your decision is final, getting comfortable in the outcome of your decision is sometimes hard to face.

Elena's Story

I remember the day I accepted the severance package. I felt overjoyed by the freedom to spend time surrounded by family. Two months passed, and I started feeling guilty since I had not considered another position in the company. Would I find another job that pays as well as my last job? Would I have enough money to send my children to college? The more I sat and thought about my decision, the more guilt I felt for not thinking beyond my severance package.

When I look back at the questions I asked myself when I accepted my severance package, I realized that all the *what if*s could not bring closure. To move out of the guilt stage, I had to look forward.

STEP 6: DEPRESSION

Now what? played over and over in my head. *Will I be able to move forward to my next venture?* I felt knocked down, and it was difficult to get up. I did not want to talk about depression because I felt it was a sign of weakness. However, depression is real when you are not sure of your next steps. Of the individuals I've mentored over the years, one individual always comes to mind.

Working for a large corporation, Joe had spent twenty years in the same department. One day his boss walked in and shared, effective immediately, his position was being phased out. The human resource representative entered the room and communicated his severance package. Joe did not hear anything the human resources person said; he had his family on his heart and mind. How would he explain his departure from the company? Numbed by the announcement, Joe slowly walked to his car. He arrived home to find his two daughters back from school. Joe tried to smile as his daughters shared their days' events, though his mind was on his next step. His wife, Laura, arrived and started dinner. Joe knew he had to tell her what happened today; on the other hand, struggled to find the right words. When the girls went to bed, Joe informed Laura that he lost his job. She was baffled by the company's decision. Joe had spent his whole career going in early, working late, and giving up special family dates for work.

The next day, Joe had a hard time getting out of bed. He did not want to talk to anyone or look for another job; he just wanted to sleep. Day after day, it was the same, *WHY? WHY ME?* Joe struggled to take any action.

The company had made a strategic move to reduce the number of employees. Months later, Joe came to grips with his termination, realizing the company's displacement decision had nothing to do with his performance.

Depression can be the lowest point in anyone's life. People might tell you, "It's not how you long you stay down, it's how quickly you get up." Consider talking to family or friends or get professional help. Time can help you mend the feeling of depression when you have support.

STEP 7: RISK

Considering the emotional impact of a transition, taking risks may be hard because of your lack of confidence in making rational choices. Perhaps fear has taken over, and you try your best to remove the feelings, but the same song of discouraging self-talk keeps playing in your head. How do you get the courage to take the risk of looking for a new job?

Stuart's Story

After successfully working for a company for five years, the company announced a reduction in force, phasing out my position. After months of hesitation, I decided to look for employment. Each interview gave me new insights into the new opportunities in the market, however the pay levels did not meet my minimum. I needed to continue to work and could not afford a cut in salary. I told myself, *Keep an open mind during your next interview.* Although the company goals and vision were different from what I was looking for, I listened to understand how my skills could help the company get to the next level. When the offer came, I struggled to take the risk of starting over in a new company, restarting my personal branding process, and embracing a new work family. Risk became an advantage when I understood one thing—I did not have a job, so what would I lose? Today, I am proud I took the leap of faith and accepted the position. The new company values my knowledge and skills, allowing me to make a difference in the new company. When you challenge yourself to take a risk, you can earn the reward of moving forward.

I took a risk and started my own company, Inspire Development, LLC. While it was and is today a lot of work, I appreciate every minute of my new business. It allows me the opportunity to set my schedule and adjust as needed. For example, at the beginning of 2020, I had finally increased the number of my speaking opportunities. Then the pandemic hit, and everything shut down. I was able to adjust by focusing more on coaching. I would not have been able to do this if I had been working for a large corporation.

STEP 8: RECOVERY

How do you recover after a significant shift in your life shakes your ego and confidence? You are told to put on your big girl panties or strap up your boots and move forward. But how? How do you shake off depression, swallow your pride, and ask for help?

My recovery was a slow one, though with time, the sun did shine again. While I was working, I had struggled to find the time to take care of myself. Also, I had often deprioritized family and friends for a workday. The transition period was a gift, a time to breathe and do something other than working sixty to eighty hours a week. I started my own consulting business and wrote two books, *Dare to Be the Change* and *Stronger Than Fear*. The process of writing these books allowed me to forgive individuals who played a part in my exiting the company and take on the next endeavor. Time also gave me the "space" to take care of myself.

The shift in my life helped me discovered my underutilized talents. I appreciate the many people who responded to my request for help, and today they continue to do so. I no longer feel fear or pride when reaching out to others because I ensure when someone asks me for help, I gladly take the time to listen and advise.

STEP 9: EMPOWERMENT

The empowerment step gives you a sense of purpose again. You may want to skip to this final step rather than going through all the steps of transition, although your path through the steps will depend on how you have tapped into your power source (e.g., family, network, religion). Sliding back and forth between the steps is normal and OK as long as the end game is to stand up and continue moving forward. Many of the individuals I have coached confided they were unhappy at work however felt remaining employed was a better option than unemployed. Yet, after they moved forward into a new venture, they felt empowerment and peace.

Empower yourself by focusing on what you can control and be open to the endless possibilities the world offers.

Humility is attentive patience

—Simone Weil

CHAPTER 3
LESSONS LEARNED THROUGH TRANSITION

I f open to change, we will learn lessons, helping us become stronger despite the change. Each experience gave me the strength to share transition advice, helping others traveling the journey. The following lessons have helped me in my journey of transition.

LESSON 1: POWERLESSNESS AND PATIENCE

When a transformation happens in an organization, the gossip grapevine usually finds out who is affected earlier than the masses. Because the individuals may not know the full or accurate story, the grapevine can cause unrest within company walls. The period of uncertainty before the official announcement requires being patient while feeling powerless because you cannot control what the company may have decided about your future.

Linda's Story

I was president of a large metro market, and I worked closely beside the chairman of the bank. One day, the holding company hired a new leader responsible for managing both of us. It quickly became apparent the company would eliminate a position due to the substantial executive level overhead. Within days, the new leader met with all my direct reports and others however never met with me. The days were long as I waited for the inevitable to happen. It took a month for management to communicate the changes. The unknown caused extreme stress. I knew, due to cost, my position was the most natural to eliminate. Feeling powerless, I had to be patient while waiting for the organization to place an offer on the table. As the saying goes, "The writing was on the wall." I had feelings of spiraling from the unknown and could not talk to anyone. The waiting period and nonexistent communication made me feel devalued. Then, finally, my last day arrived. Sitting in my office, the new leader shared the news of eliminating my position. It was a five-minute meeting, and the only question asked was, "What do you spend your time doing during the day?" I quickly made a list of my duties. Soon after, the human resources representative walked into the room. While the representative went over the severance package, I struggled to control my emotions and remain professional. Then, the human resources representative asked me to leave and come back in the afternoon to pack my office. *Leave and come back? No!* I quickly gathered a few personal items and my purse, leaving never to return.

Waiting for thirty days and not knowing the direction of the company made me feel powerless. After the notification, I felt relieved. I could plan my new path.

Lesson learned: How do you conquer the feeling of powerlessness? Let go of the internal struggle of trying to convince yourself it's not your position being phased out. Instead, use your energy to think about your next career step and take the power back from individuals who give you doubts.

LESSON 2: TAKE TIME FOR YOU

During my working years, I missed many family opportunities. Even though I went on vacation many times, I worked in between family time. I never prioritized time for me.

When my shift from the financial world happened, I entered a space of not knowing what to do next. I struggled to find my purpose. I felt concerned about whether I should find another job in the same arena or a different field altogether. This loud mental noise reinforced my uncertainty. I needed time to clear my mind before making any decisions.

My husband understood the need to "take time for you." On the day of the reorganization announcement, he immediately booked four trips. On the last day of work with my bags packed, I took off to our first destination. No computer, no projects due, and I agreed to let him answer my phone. He understood my need to confide in someone and rest. He scheduled a visit with my best friend, Patrick. Patrick acknowledged what had happened and did not judge my decisions. We laughed about the past times and talked about the future. I was able to sleep again and not worry about the fallout from the announcement.

Lesson learned: Take the time to read a book, go to the movies, visit a friend, or sit on the back porch and enjoy the song of the birds and the whistle of the wind. Remember, you will never be able to replace the time to reflect and clear your mind before moving to the next venture. It's your time to *breathe*.

LESSON 3: TAKE CARE OF YOURSELF

I often say, "I want to be surrounded by people who give coins, not take coins away." Seek people who have a positive attitude and will increase your energy level. During the period of change, you feel many emotions. Consider being around people who support you. When you do take care of yourself, you boost your immune system.

During my first week of separation from my company, I did not take care of myself. I ate everything I loved, including ice cream, dark chocolate, and, oh yes, lots of fried foods. Six months later, I had gained twenty pounds. I had learned bad eating habits during my many years of traveling and never took the time to workout. Always exhausted when the day ended, I found a few minutes to grab a quick bite, shower, review emails, and eventually go to bed to repeat the cycle day after day—not a great plan for longevity. To change my eating behavior, I joined a weight loss program. While I am supportive of such programs, unless you have the mindset to do something about your weight, changes will not happen. Also, I had high blood pressure, which, thankfully, medication controlled. I decided to exercise and maintain a healthy diet to keep me from derailing.

I found an affordable gym near my home. The gym provided the classes, equipment, and structure for success. I set a goal of exercising a minimum of five days a week and a goal of eating healthier. I ate more green vegetables and fruits, and I no longer ate fast foods on the go. I also needed a motivational partner to keep me on course. My husband, a former football player, set the example of getting up every morning and making health our top priority. During the first week of exercising, my muscles ached, and I did not see the results immediately. However, I went back day after day until working out became a daily habit. Healthy living became my new job. Also, the routine of exercising helped me clear my mind. I eventually made friends at the gym and surrounded myself with people who gave me energy and supported me. When I started feeling guilty about missing a class, I knew I had graduated to healthy living for life.

Gladys's Story

After working for over twenty years, including while on vacation or sick, I found myself amid a company reduction in force. As my manager shared the news of my departure with the team, I felt my chest tighten. I silently gathered my box of belongings. I hugged all of my teammates and ensured I would stay in touch. When I arrived home, my daughter saw I was having difficulty breathing. My daughter immediately called 911. A heart attack! It took me months to overcome the effects of the heart attack, still I recovered with help from family and friends. Today, I tell my story as a lesson in taking care of yourself by eating the right foods and exercising. Do not wait for an event like a heart attack to wake up and improve your health.

Lesson learned: We move as swiftly as the wind and struggle to slow down, breathe, and take care of ourselves. Be strong and ensure you have a healthy body and mind. Focus on activities that will improve your health. Stay active (e.g., exercise, non-profit work, mentoring) to keep you motivated to improve your health. Keeping busy will help you shift your negative thoughts to doing something meaningful.

LESSON 4: DETERMINE YOUR KEY SOURCES OF SUPPORT

When a transition happens, we prefer to hide away from the world. We ask, *Why?* We feel inadequate as we enter the abyss of the unknown. We look for answers, yet clouds block the sun. We attempt to stand, though something in our core will not let us.

To overcome these feelings, plug into your power source. Where do you get your power? Perhaps your spiritual practice, coach, family, network, physical activity, or time helping others are your power sources.

I am blessed to have my family as a power source. They listened, they did not judge me, and they supported me throughout my career. They helped me see that facing my fear could be an advantage.

A coach can help you identify your strengths. Many individuals I coached on fear were not initially aware of their strengths however were always quick to discuss their weaknesses. A coach can partner with you to help you tap into your own power.

Pay your blessings forward by finding the time to mentor others. This will increase your *own* power.

When you face fear, surround yourself with individuals supportive of your journey. Though they may not fully understand, they will help you get through the difficult days. Stay away from individuals who ask "why" and only want to share gossip they heard from others. The greatest joy of a taking person (versus a giving person) is reporting to others your current disposition.

I once worked with a coworker who thrived on finding out other employees' personal business. The coworker spent their days talking on the phone or ensuring to sit at the right lunch table. If anything of importance happened in the company, they worked hard to get the information. Surrounding yourself with "taking" individuals will extract energy versus restore energy.

If family and friends are not available as a source of support, find a group in which you feel comfortable sharing your feelings. Do not spend time alone. A friend of mine believed he did not need support when he received the news of separation. He felt ashamed, and he continued to push his family and friends away. While many suggested he pursue help, he smiled and said, "I got this." One day he woke up and had difficulty speaking. He soon found himself in the emergency room. After a couple of hours in the emergency room, the doctor shared the bad news. A stroke! Now paralyzed, his priority was no longer getting the next job interview, only one goal: to get better. He tells how his family and friends were the first to arrive at the hospital to help him. They did not judge him and just wanted to support him.

Lesson learned: Ask yourself, "Who are my power sources?" Reach out to them. Remember, many people want to help you.

LESSON 5: WHEN YOUR FRIENDS DO NOT CALL

I always considered my "work family" my second family. My network in the finance industry had grown over the years to hundreds of colleagues. However, after the announcement of my leaving, only a few close friends called. In your time of need, some may feel uneasy to talk to you for many reasons:

- They do not know what to say to you.
- They worry someone from the company will discover their connection to you and endanger their job.
- Your appeal to others may have been your title or position, which you no longer have.

Unfortunately, many of those you expect to hear from will not call.

I had worked for the company for over fourteen years. I knew I had strong relationships during my tenure in the company, now I questioned why I did not hear from some of my close friends. One day I called one of the associates I had not heard from since my departure. I wanted to check in on her, yet I also wanted to ask why I did not hear from her. Her response shook me to my core. "I did not call you because I feared being placed on the next transition list." Our discussion helped me see others' points of view and how fear causes individuals to do what feels hurtful.

About six months later, I received a call from a young man whom I had mentored over the years. He started by apologizing for not calling sooner and also admitted his fear of calling. A peer had told him if he called me, he might make the next transition list. *What? Talking to me would put his job in jeopardy? Why would anyone communicate a message instilling fear in others? Is management afraid transitioned individuals will speak negatively about the company to current employees? Does the guilt of pushing someone out make a person look for ways to feel better, or is it about control?*

I coached a client experiencing friends not calling. She had worked with several close colleagues for over ten years. Every morning, she looked forward to coffee and conversation with them. She considered her colleagues her best friends because they had helped her through many difficult personal issues. As a senior leader, she was the person everyone went to for advice. She had helped many when their supervisor did not understand the issue. For example, an employee had designed a new system that would save the company money. She took the program and piloted it in her department and then presented it to the company's executives. She was a champion for the underdog. Now no longer employed, she could not understand why they did not call her to check on her. While she understood she was no longer viewed as an asset, she also felt rejected as a friend. Are friendships formed because of your title, position, or network of individuals within your circle, rather than your compatibility with the person? *Now What?*

Recently, when the floods of Hurricane Harvey damaged the Texas coast, everyone went into help mode. Neighbors helped neighbors, and strangers helped strangers. After a few months of helping, it seemed to become old news. Yet, two years later, the effects of the storm are still with many Texas residents. The same happens when you experience a critical life change. In the first couple of weeks, you hear from lots of people who are concerned about your well-being, want to know what happened, or ask whether they are next on the list. However, after a few weeks, the phone stops ringing except for a few individuals.

Lesson learned: Seek support from friends and family who nurture your well-being beyond work. Unless you forge a stronger "work family" relationship outside of work, it will probably be a more distant relationship than you think. Commit to spending more time surrounded by your closest family and friends.

LESSON 6: JOURNAL YOUR THOUGHTS

Disconnecting from work was difficult. I loved the work and the people I had worked beside for many years. I had never considered myself a writer nonetheless started writing my thoughts after I read writing coach Tom Bird's book, *Write to Heal.* Journaling my thoughts about my transition helped me forgive myself and others I had blamed for the displacement. Writing also brought closure to my hurt feelings from my job loss and put an end to my mind's negative self-dialogue.

Mind mapping may be a good activity to help you journal. Start by making a large circle on a sheet of blank, unruled paper. In the middle of that circle, write the name of the person, event, or situation that distresses you. Then quickly draw smaller circles around the large circle, inserting words describing your feelings about it. Continue the process until you cannot think of another word. For example, write the word, "transition" in the large circle. In the smaller circles, write the words, "shock," "identity," "fear," "angry," "confused," or any other words associated with the main word, "transition."

You will know when to stop once the words stop flowing. Then take the words and write why you feel this way. For example: Powerless—I did not initiate the decision to transition from the workplace. Then continue to write until you no longer feel angry and you have exhausted the emotions.

Lesson learned: Journaling helped me close the chapter of transition and freed me from feeling like a victim. Consider writing for fifteen minutes daily. Do not think about what to write—write what comes to your mind.

LESSON 7: HUMANS ARE WIRED TO WORK

We are wired to strive, grow, and contribute our best to something bigger than ourselves, to be useful, and to do meaningful work. Work not only allows us to take care of ourselves and our families, work also gives us a sense of autonomy, focus, and routine. It is fundamental to our identity and confidence.

Work is so integral to our lives that it can feel shocking and disorienting when a transition happens. Like a tidal wave, the cornerstone of our daily lives'—the routines, responsibilities, and relationships—are swept away. Beyond a sense of purpose and direction and the real or perceived lost and the ability to take care of what we care about, we can only watch the world as we knew it drift further and further out of sight. The disruption to our lives and sense of self is staggering.

Transitions are always doorways to change. Even under the best of conditions, change is challenging. The future doesn't come with a roadmap, and the route to your next destination is only visible in hindsight. The first few steps into the unknown often release chaos on two fronts: a crisis of identity and a crisis of confidence. When the transition isn't your choice, this duo of doubt can leave you feeling powerless and alone, locked in an emotional jail without the keys. While not always obvious, you do have the keys to free yourself—and take the first steps on your next adventure.

According to the creators of the Personalysis personality assessment, everyone has two sets of keys: one is universal, and one is unique to you.

THE UNIVERSAL KEY

The body is the universal key everyone has to getting their bearings. The tidal waves of emotion can be overwhelming, and you may react in ways that seem out of character for days or weeks or even longer. That's normal. Telling yourself to snap out of it often doesn't work and can add to your stress. Here are a few things that might help:

- Stand-up: When our confidence collapses, our body does as well. Fortunately, our bodies can not only reflect but also shift our emotions. Focus on standing up, really straight and tall. Pull your shoulders back and your chin up. Notice what happens.

- Breathe: Breathing can be a powerful mood shifter. When overwhelm and anxiety can seem like constant companions, take a few deep breaths. Inhale through your nose slowly and deeply and exhale slowly. Do this for thirty seconds—and notice what happens.

- Reach out: Loneliness and isolation are two of the biggest challenges of transition. While counterintuitive, reaching out to others in transition is one of the most powerful things you can do. Find job search groups in your area (or your area of interest), and rather than look for ways the group can help you, look for ways to help and encourage others.

THE CUSTOM KEY

Transition is a self-awareness learning lab. The experience will change you, and you will discover and deepen your understanding of many facets of yourself. Learning about your unique personality can not only help you in your career going forward and can also be a key to confidence in the short-term.

There are many tools to help you, yet I have found the Personalysis Profile at https://personalysis.wiredto-thrive.com to be especially effective in helping people discover the keys to help unlock their confidence. It is the inspiration for the four confidence keys outlined below. While you may find that a single key below works for you, many people find a combination of these keys opens the door to clarity and confidence.

Key #1: Direction and Focus

If you gain confidence when you have a clear goal and can draw on your experience to take action toward it, Direction and Focus may be one of your confidence keys. You are likely to rely on these to avoid distractions and build momentum. Without a purpose, a plan, or experience in the job search domain, your natural tendency to try harder to find a way through the fog of overwhelm can prevent you from moving forward. You may bounce from action to action or develop tunnel-vision and focus all your energy in a single direction, only to discover you have been spinning your wheels. To unlock your confidence and start making progress:

- Set one goal for today—something you can accomplish or learn how to do—and do it.
- Start small and record your activity.
- Set a goal for one action each day for a week. At the end of the week, review the activity log and the progress you made. Repeat the process next week.

Key #2: Collaboration and Support

If you feel clearer and more confident when you are working with others, moving forward together to achieve a goal, Collaboration and Support may be one of the keys to your confidence. You tend to be optimistic and flexible, explore a variety of options, and try new ways of doing things. In transition, you no longer have access to two important sources of confidence: the flow of work and the support and encouragement of others. Without their support, it is easy to become isolated, unfocused, and overwhelmed. You may try to compensate by throwing yourself into networking or chasing one new possibility after another. If you are busy and not getting closer to your goal, it's time to do something different. To unlock your confidence and start making progress:

- Find one or two networking groups and show up.
- Join, or even form, a small group of job seekers who work together to support, encourage, and help each other in the job search process.

- Get curious, meet regularly, and bring out and leverage each person's strengths to support each other. By creating and nurturing these new relationships, you expand your confidence and your ability to discover more new possibilities that are a good fit for you.

Key #3: Purpose and Strategy

If you feel more confident when you have a clear sense of purpose, context, and direction, Purpose and Strategy may be one of your confidence keys. While seeking various perspectives and thinking through multiple scenarios can help you gain clarity in transition. Doing exhaustive research looking for answers often will keep you stuck in a mental tailspin. To unlock your confidence and start making progress:

- Focus on a directional goal and look for ways to move toward it.
- Focusing on the why you are taking action and experiment, conceptual solutions don't move you forward.
- Another booster: Find one or two collaborators and tap into each other's strengths. You can be sounding boards, coaches, and confidants to challenge assumptions and deepen each other's thinking. Watch a new future emerge as you do.

Key #4: Plan and Process

If having a concrete goal, a reliable plan, and the ability to take proven action to achieve it, Plan and Process may be one of your confidence keys. Before you move forward, identify and analyze the potential risks and build a map to avoid as many risks as possible. In transition, the existing plans for the future vanish, taking your confidence with it. When you don't have a specific goal or outcome, how do you create a plan to achieve success? Sorting through conflicting advice about navigating in transition, identifying where to start, the steps you need to take—in what order— is more overwhelming. With so many options and unknowns, your brain gets stuck and you struggle to see any path forward.

To unlock your confidence and start making progress:

- Set a goal. Not a huge stretch goal, a goal to help you move forward in a specific way.
- Sort through data and choose the next three actions to get moving. Repeat that process, make adjustments, and track your progress. Soon you will plot a roadmap to success.

Ella's Story

My personality is direction and focus. The day the company closed its doors, over six hundred employees left the company. All the associates went home, though I felt I needed to remain in the company to finalize the financial books. After all, I am the chief financial officer. Staying in the company is the only way to protect my brand and to ensure the closure through the end. I did not have time to grieve because I needed to work alongside the attorneys, bankers, and vendors.

About a year before the closure, my boss had sought investors to buy the company. Doubting his abilities, he hired a senior leader possessing top credentials. His plan to woo a potential buyer required presenting the company not only as financially sound but also as having leaders with highly sought-after credentials. After a brief chat, I knew the new leader did not care about our culture. He had no substance in his business dialogue and only talked in bumper sticker quotes. I immediately shared my concerns with my boss, however he discounted my input. Just under one year later, the company failed.

The day after the announcement, I walked back into a quiet and empty office. I felt angry, numb, depressed, and disenchanted. After all my warnings, we had failed. As a result, I no longer respected my boss. He also tried to destroy my brand by blaming me for the downfall of the company. I decided I would stand on the word "perseverance" and manage what I could control. I focused on my health and lost seventy pounds. Each day, I went home emotionally and physically drained. I worked day in and day out alongside CPAs, bankers, and the bankruptcy court until we closed all the books.

Months went by. Embarrassed to share the bankruptcy status of the company, I became more reserved. However, I knew I needed to work and prove to myself that I am capable of doing a great job.

My most significant learning through the separation was that the company did not need me as much as I needed them. Another learning was to believe in myself because I am the only person controlling my actions.

We all have all four confidence keys—Direction and Focus, Collaboration and Support, Purpose and Strategy, and Plan and Process. We lean most on our core, our top two personality types. My top two confidence keys are: Direction and Focus and Plan and Process. To gain self-confidence, I needed to do several things in alignment with my dominant personality types. First, I needed to see the endpoint. Second, I required structure, a plan to control the risk. My return to normal included my daily list of things to do; I would check off each item completed and update the list continuously. I joined non-profit organizations giving me purpose. I took time to *breathe*.

Lesson learned: Once you've lost your purpose, routines, relationships, and identity, how do you pick yourself up? To regain your confidence, learn about your confidence keys to help you focus on your strengths. Know that you aren't (and hopefully will never become) an expert at job transition, whereas it can become one of the most valuable learning experiences of your life. Finally, breathe.

LESSON 8: UPDATE YOUR RESUME AND SOCIAL MEDIA INFORMATION

When someone works in a job they love, losing passion never enters their mind. They work day and night to accomplish their goals and projects. When headhunters call, they dismiss the exchange. When an unexpected transition occurs, they rush to update their resume and social media information. Some employers pass them to an outplacement company. The outplacement company helps update resumes not necessarily social media. A person's years of service or position in the company determines how much the company will help them transition, if at all.

While I was still in the corporate world, I never updated my resume unless for a new opportunity, which did not happen often. Fortunately, part of the severance package I received included updating my resume and six months of coaching. I also spent time understanding the interview process. One prospective employer, I first completed an online application. Then I phone interviewed with the recruiting representative. Next, I sent in a video of a mock teaching scenario. The company liked the video and invited me to a three-hour networking event to see how I interacted with other applicants and office staff. Finally, I met the company's interview panel. Not all companies have the same process, so familiarize yourself with the interview process of each company you are interested in.

Amazingly, I did not think about the importance of LinkedIn, Facebook, Twitter, Instagram, or other social media sites. When I started looking for employment,

I realized that if someone wanted to get to know me, they would first look at my social media information.

Lesson learned: Update your resume and social media information annually, whether looking for a job or not. Take the time to discuss hiring processes with friends, colleagues, or your company's Human Resources department. If you're uncomfortable using technology, find someone to help you navigate social media sites.

LESSON 9: BUILD A STRONG NETWORK

After returning from my trip to visit my friend, Patrick, I gathered all my contacts from social media, excel spreadsheets, and my phone. The list of hundreds of names included individuals I had met at events, clients, and other acquaintances. My previous definition of a contact was a chat or a brief conversation.

After many years in the customer service world, the hours of training, and the many networking events, did I understand the meaning of a business relationship? My definition of a business relationship applied to individuals in my "book of business," but had I established personal relationships with them beyond the business world? Also, had my association with my contacts become stagnant?

In addition, I had decided to start my own business as an executive coach. I started asking myself whether my definition of a contact applied to my new role.

When I evaluated my list of contacts relative to my new identity as a coach and small business owner, the list suddenly withered to less than fifty names. Horrified by my discovery, I concluded I needed to rebuild my network.

I started with the first person on my list. I emailed asking we meet for coffee to update them on my new ventures. As always, I arrived early at the restaurant and ordered a cup of coffee. About five minutes later, my friend joined me. We shared our family updates, and I shared my vision for my new company. My friend offered to help but unsure whether her connections in the corporate world would employ a one-person business. Many large corporations use coaching firms that offer coaches at several levels (e.g., executive, wellness, leadership). My company only employed one: me. I got the same reaction from many people in my network.

When I looked back at my career and tried to pinpoint where I went wrong, I struggled with the answer. Yes, I network, however did I develop a relationship? Consider expanding your network to help your next employment possibility.

I recently met a lady at a luncheon, we exchanged cards, and as usual, I placed the card in my wallet and forgot about the exchange. One day, I came across a corporation I wanted to submit a speaking proposal to. Then I remembered the lady, pulled out the card, and set up a fifteen-minute Zoom call. I learn about her both personally and professionally, and she also connected me to her supervisor at the corporation. While working, I did not take the time to communicate beyond the business card consistently. Now, I pause and make it a priority.

Imagine looking for a job and knowing someone who worked for the company in which you are interested. If you met them, say, four years ago, how do you reconnect if you did not establish a connection early on? I no longer take business cards for granted; I take the time to get to know the individual personally.

Lesson learned: When you meet someone and exchange a business card, follow up by setting up a fifteen-minute get-to-know-you call to find out a little more about the individual personally. It is time well spent. Also consider keeping a spreadsheet of notes. The information may open doors for future connections. Build a network of individuals you know personally and find ample resources when you decide to take the next journey in your career.

Lesson 10: Do Not Take the First Job

You are likely shocked after the news of your potential unemployment. Some of my coaching clients say:

"I must find another job, now!"

"I cannot sit home all day."

"After a routine of working outside the home, I need contact with other people."

"It does not matter what the job entails; I just need to work."

Unfortunately, some take the first job available to them. Once in the workplace, they know immediately they have made a mistake, and the new job is not their passion. They also take the risk their employer might find out their unhappiness as they continue to look for other opportunities.

When I started looking for my next job, my age caused me some apprehension. My executive coach encouraged me to find a job before I turned sixty years old. What? I have over *forty years* in the business. Why does age matter? I have the energy of someone many years younger. I was fifty-nine years old, and the clock ticked loudly. After applying for every job online or referred to me, I finally stopped the madness of trying to just get a job. Finding my next chapter required me to assess my passion for the next chapter of my working years. I pondered the sustainability of working days of twelve or fourteen hours. Fearful of failure, I continued to interview. The more I interviewed, the more I was turned down, primarily for being overqualified. When I wasn't overqualified, the salary did not meet my minimum expectations. However, I knew taking the first job would only keep me looking for the perfect job. In the end, I took a risk and started my own company. Owning my business helped me bring balance back into my life and spend more time with family.

Too many highly skilled individuals will settle for just a job because they need income or insurance or because they fear boredom. However, once they accept the position, many soon discover that the job does not meet their expectations. Interviewing and training wasted their time and energy. Why not stop, take a deep breath, and use your network and resources to find the right job?

Lesson learned: You want to be happy and content for the next five, ten, or more years. To ensure peace in your core, take your time, and find the right job. If a company expects a twelve-hour day, yet you know eight hours is your maximum, do not take the job—it does not match your values. A job is not just a job; it has to be your passion because you spend much of your waking hours working.

LESSON 11: BE TRUE TO YOUR VALUES

I always thought I was true to my values until Jerry shared his transition story.

Jerry's Story

Wow, I just lost my job, I thought. The word *end* kept going through my head. It's the end of a steady income, the end of managing a team, and the end of my livelihood. I had worked in the corporate world for over thirty years. I had always prided myself on being a quiet person, excelling in my position, and working sixty-hour workweeks.

The morning after my final workday, I watched my wife leave for work. Alone with our dog, Astro, I felt I should be getting ready for work, planning my day, or doing something productive. One side of me felt relieved, free from the ongoing meetings, the employee relations issues, and the rushing to and from meetings. The other side of me worried, *What am I going to do now?*

My new beginning took a long time because I stayed in the end state for months. Every day I woke up and buried myself in grief. I replayed the past, asking what I could have done differently. I felt sorry for myself instead of thinking of myself as free—free from the long hours and, more importantly, free to explore new possibilities. How could I look at my separation from the company differently?

First, I disconnected from everyone. I took time for myself and traveled to clear my head and rediscover myself. I did not want to hear about my unemployment from family and friends. Being too close to the experience, I had conflicting thoughts about the advice they gave me. I needed to mourn. Every time someone called, texted, or emailed me, my wound reopened, and I bled grief.

Traveling gave me time for clarity for my next step, including making time for hobbies. I started volunteering for a non-profit organization. Once I started doing something different, I saw another world beyond work. I also concluded that I had chosen my lifestyle. I closed the chapter of hurt in my book.

When I decided to go back to work, I promised myself I would approach work differently. My next job would be under my terms. I would refuse relocations, focus on my health, and ensure the company culture and values aligned with mine. When I looked back, I recognized I had prostituted my values. When I did not agree with management's decisions, I had remained silent to avoid making waves. Now, I have learned to be selfish in a good way. I have learned to be me.

Time helped me understand I was my biggest enemy. I fully understand why the mind trains you to think *the end*. Allow yourself to walk the stages of transition from the end to the beginning of a new chapter.

Like Jerry, I also had betrayed my standards by agreeing to company decisions that ultimately kept me up at night, regretting my agreement.

Lesson Learned: In my transition journey, I learned to forgive myself for these past mistakes and, like Jerry, I am committed to being more authentic in my agreements. When you find yourself questioning others' decisions, always trust your instincts and never override your core values.

By failing to prepare, you are preparing to fail.

—Benjamin Franklin

CHAPTER 4
WHAT WOULD YOU DO DIFFERENTLY?

In my coaching interviews with individuals experiencing a departure from the workplace, I always include the question, "What would you do differently, if anything?" While many of the responses differ, one remains the same. "I no longer put work first; my family is now my focus."

One friend shared, "Sometimes we do not realize we've attached ourselves intravenously to the drug of work. We robotically get up in the morning and do the same job day in and day out, not thinking change can happen in a moment's notice."

Another friend said, "I have learned my value is more significant than the work I do or my job title."

Since 2015, I have coached many individuals through their transition from the workplace. While it is a difficult journey, we can rise above it with the right support. Jerry's advice is, "Consider not tackling the venture alone." The event can make you question your value as a human and erode your confidence. Do not isolate yourself. Do not take the first job immediately, since your insecurity could be driving the decision. Also, take time off and enjoy aspects of life you may not have had time for while employed. Invest in yourself.

A transition gives you a chance to breathe and know tomorrow, the sun will rise, and you will go through the change. Do not rush to enter your next chapter. Remember, your mind may have many clouds of confusion. Give time to clear the shadows. You will know when it's the right time to move forward.

Empty your mind. Be formless, shapeless like water. Now you put water into a cup, it becomes the cup. You put water into a bottle, it becomes the bottle. You put water in a teapot, it becomes the teapot. Now water can flow or it can crash. Be water my friend.

—Bruce Lee

CHAPTER 5
MANAGE CHANGE BEFORE A TRANSITION HAPPENS

Every year automation increases, replacing the need for a physical body to do the job. We continue to see companies reduce the number of employees. To ensure not being blindsided by a disruption in your career, first remain relevant in the workplace. Second, step back and reevaluate whether you have prepared for an unforeseen change in the workplace.

Liz's Story

I consider myself a passionate person in both work and family. Work is a critical part of who I am. Similar to a marriage, it has its ups and downs. I fell in love with my job, the employees, and the company. In my ten years of working, I had always received above average or superior performance review ratings. Many valued my competencies and sought me for advice or to work on company projects, mentor employees, or lead a new initiative. I had won many awards, including vacation trips for my sales performance. I felt invincible.

Then one day, an all-hands meeting gave me the news: I no longer had a job. *What? Did they just say my name? They made a mistake!* I wanted to walk out of the room and call the head of my department to correct the error. As I asked questions, no one took ownership of the *why*. If not for low performance or competency, then what? They started telling me to use the severance package to remodel my house, travel, or move closer to my husband's job. I sat speechless. I felt as if my husband had filed for divorce. I kept thinking, *You have taken away my livelihood, my love.* Disheartened, I no longer felt invincible. I became a number, no different from anyone else losing their job.

Losing my job humbled me. I do not take anything for granted. Now I no longer tell a headhunter "no" to an interview. I stay connected with my resources. Today, I have a new job, though I look at the role differently. I focus on developing myself beyond the position by staying healthy and not working 24/7. I learned a valuable lesson that I am more than a job or title.

Cary's Story

October 16, 2019, a day I will never forget. It was a typical day. I got up at 4:00 a.m. to ensure enough time to meet the van that drove some employees to the office. We arrived at work at 6:30 a.m., the first to arrive at the office, ready to assist customers. These colleagues are like a second family to me. After thirty-five years of working in the industry, I loved working with people and numbers; I called it my happy job.

After an hour at the job, my director came by and asked to see me in her office. I replied, "Sure." We proceeded down the hallway yet did not turn toward her office. I thought, "This is odd," as we continued to the executive level floor and went into a conference room. Sitting at the table was the vice president and the human resource partner. Having previously worked in human resources, I knew what was going to happen next. The human resource partner was in tears. The vice president said that the company was going through a transformation. Deciding to reduce staff was hard, and downsizing was the only option. After thirty-five years, my company eliminated my job.

Previously, the company had offered a voluntary retirement package. I had not taken the severance package because I had seen many staff reductions in the past and never thought that there would be additional downsizing. Considered a model employee, I had recently received a company award. The human resources partner went over the early retirement package, which included severance and medical. I was in complete shock, yet I tried to remain professional.

My next instructions were to pack up my office—a lifetime of memories. My co-workers stopped by my desk to express their disbelief. I placed thirty-five years of my life into *six boxes.*

The administrative assistant offered to take me to my car. I loaded up my six boxes and said my goodbyes. I felt as if I was in a dream. *Would someone please wake me up? This cannot be happening.* I kept telling myself, *Remain positive. Being negative won't help anyone.* I thought of how I would always sing the song "You Are My Sunshine" to my children when they were in elementary school. I knew there would be sunshine again, though I did not see sunshine now.

When I arrived home, I told my husband and children. They were all surprised because they knew how hard I worked for the company and that it was an important part of my life. I called my sister, and she said that she would help me update my resume and profile. She understood because October 16 was a noteworthy day in her life. She had gone through the same process five years ago, on the same date.

After leaving a company where I had spent over three decades, what does the word "transition" mean? I have gone through every kind of emotion from anger, hurt, fear, sadness, and finally, acceptance. How could this happen to a loyal, hardworking person who believed in the goodness of humanity?

There were many days that I felt I was in a dream and thought, *Please wake me up!* However, I have since learned that a job does not define who I am as a person. It can only enhance who I can become. A *fog* is how I sum up my transition period. The fog will disappear, and I have faith that there will be clearer days ahead.

The stories of these seemingly untouchable all-stars being transitioned out of their companies prove this can happen to anyone. Manage the change before an unexpected transition happens. Some areas to consider while working are: Network, Resume, Social Media, and Key Sources of Support.

NETWORK

Make a list of your professional contacts. These are individuals you value and respect, who you would consider working alongside in the future.

1. Separate the individuals by how well you know them using the below chart.

A	Strong personal relationship (e.g., you'd ask each other for personal advice)
B	Weak personal relationship (e.g., you interact outside of work)
C	No personal relationship (e.g., you exchanged business cards without follow-up or interact only at work)

2. Once you have divided your contacts into these groups, focus on the A list. Set a target of how many individuals you would like to contact daily. Reach out by email, social media, or telephone, or set up a videoconference or in-person meeting. Ask for help—people want to make connections for you. It gives them a sense of helping others.

3. Establish an ongoing follow-up system to stay in contact. Reach out to say hello or happy birthday. When your next opportunity avails itself, your network will be your power source.

4. Continue to reassess your network list. Is there anyone you should reconnect with from your B list? How often should you follow up—monthly, semiannually, annually?

5. Consider working two or three contacts from your C list monthly.

RESUME

Update your resume every six months or annually. When we have our heads down working, updating our resume is not our top priority. Keeping a resume current will save you time when seeking other employment. Resumes tell your future employer your story in skills and competencies. If your company does not give you the chance to work with an outplacement center, you have several options to consider. First, you can find sample resumes online, giving you insight into what employers look for in a candidate. Once you have written your draft resume, seek a resume editor to ensure your resume speaks to the job of interest. Second, contact a coach specializing in helping individuals in a career transition. Last, ask for help from your network.

SOCIAL MEDIA

Update your social media sites, especially LinkedIn. A current professional photo is your first step to updating your site. When recruiters source for candidates, your photo helps tell the recruiter your personal brand. Use the same photo on all your sites (e.g., Facebook, Instagram, etc.). Second, contact individuals you have worked alongside in the past and request they write a recommendation for your LinkedIn page. Third, consider listing your current position as "Open to opportunities." Or consider a status update such as, "Currently seeking employment." Include the field of interest (e.g., financial, retail, etc.). Fourth, share your professional expertise in your headline. For example, write "Leadership Coach," "Small Business Lender," or "Speaker."

KEY SOURCES OF SUPPORT

Determine your key sources of support. For example, my list includes spiritual practice, family, coach, exercise, or helping others. Write specific goals for each source.

- Spiritual practice: I go to church every Sunday. I find getting involved in the church activities gave me the family support needed, especially during a difficult time.

- Family: I have three sisters, two of whom live in another state, and the phone is our best communication tool to stay connected. Once a month, I travel to Louisiana to visit in person.

- Coach: I have committed to helping individuals going through a transition from work. Consider contacting a coach to help you through the first three months or longer.

- Exercise: I changed my behavior to take care of myself. Now, my routine is working out four to five days a week. Start by walking thirty minutes a day. You will see an improvement in your physical and mental state.

- Helping others: I continue to teach financial literary classes, whether through the non-profit Greater Houston Women's Resource or private one-on-one. What a great feeling in giving back to my community.

Start today, one step at a time. Your sources of support will embrace helping you through tough days.

UNDERSTAND YOUR BEHAVIOR

As previously shared in Chapter 3, the four confidence keys are: Direction and Focus, Collaboration and Support, Purpose and Strategy, and Plan and

Process. Write a specific activity you can do each week or month. For example, my primary confidence keys are Direction and Focus and Plan and Process. I needed structure and understanding of the big picture. I continue to use daily lists, and I researched topics of interest.

Sometimes it's family and friends that put you back on track. Other personality types require that you take on a project that will give you a focus. Understanding your personality will help you move quicker through the transition stages. Also, consider taking a personality assessment.

JOURNAL YOUR THOUGHTS

Start your day scheduling fifteen minutes for you. Find a quiet area and take the time to write your feelings. Sometimes the emotion will be anger; other times, you may have a great memory of something from the past. Whatever it is, write it down, enjoy the emotion, and continue to write daily to purge your negative emotions. Writing helped me forgive myself and others. It also helped me close chapters and write a new chapter.

FINAL THOUGHTS

Recently a friend asked me, "Why was your transition from work hard?" As I started to answer the question, memories of the displacement flooded back like a river. I saw myself sitting in the boardroom, discussing my separation from the company. I remember the hurt feelings of my company viewing me as a number rather than a person. I had felt unrecognized for all my past contributions. Blinded by the fog in my head, my emotions had taken over; my crying had continued for days. I had struggled with the finality of forty years of a passion. As I told my friend my story, I still missed the work and my associates and friends. I felt free—free to smile and know I made it through a tough time.

When I receive a call from someone who is losing their job, I want to tell them immediately, "You will be okay," yet I know not everyone reacts the same to a transition. Instead, I listen and offer assistance. I also send a note similar to the one a friend sent me during my challenging time. Below is part of the note I received:

A transition from a career you loved can be stressful. You may feel a sense of loss, maybe some humiliation, and anxiety about the unknown future. There is some excitement and anticipation about creating a new chapter.

As you go through this period, consider:

- *Notice how you feel at the moment. Do not judge or make the feeling wrong. Acknowledge your feeling of the moment. Write your feelings down because writing has the positive impact of resetting the mind. Remember, it's your feeling, and you are entitled to it. Notice the changes in your emotions as the transition progresses. Do not panic if it gets harder before it gets better.*

- *Who are you throughout the process? All transitions can be traumatic, some more than others. My mantra is "move with ease and grace." I meditate on these words every spare moment. It has helped me remain calm and clears my head to make the right decisions.*

- *Last, a transition is wonderful—it has given you freedom to start something new and enable you to change for a better life.*

Throughout the first three months of my transition, my husband said that I needed to embrace my own advice that I was bravely sharing with others who were struggling with their transition. I am quick to help someone else but could not seem to help myself. I wanted to shout, "This is not fair; I am a good person. Why me?" Instead, I sat on the back porch and cried for days, not wanting to see anyone. I undoubtedly had to purge all the negative dialogue in my head. I know now crying is what I needed to do. So, cry, shout, or do whatever feels right for you. Today, I am enjoying my time with my best friend, my husband. We have traveled to places I always dreamed of visiting. I am teaching leadership classes, am invited to speak at various events, and taking care of myself. You will be okay—travel the pilgrimage of learning and accept the gifts of growth. You will be better off for the blessing of transition and you can now answer the question-*Now What?*

Notes & Bibliography

1. "A New View of Personality: Dynamic Distinctions." Personalysis. 2021. Mar 17, 2021. https://personalysis. wiredtothrive.com/assessment/.

ABOUT THE AUTHOR

Annella Metoyer is a performance improvement coach specializing in enhancing executives' leadership skills so they can dare to "be the change" in their growing organizations. With over thirty-five years of solving complex problems and building high-performance teams in the finance industry, Annella today coaches business leaders to understand personality types and behavioral skills that create strategic results.

Annella passionately serves on the boards of many professional and non-profit organizations, including Gulf Copper, Jack Brooks Foundation, North Houston

Advisory Board of the Greater Houston Women's Chamber of Commerce (GHWCC), and the Women's Resource of Greater Houston.

She has also served on the board of the Greater Houston Partnership and the 2011 NCAA Final Four Houston Local Organizing Committee. The International Association of Top Professionals named Annella the 2019 Top Motivational Speaker of the Year and the 2020 Lifetime Achievement Award. The Greater Houston Women's Chamber of Commerce named Annella as one of its "Breakthrough Women" of 2013. In 2012, Annella was among the honorees at the 7th Annual Top 25 Women of Houston Awards. Annella was also named as one of Houston's "50 Most Influential Women for 2011" by the readers and staff of Houston Woman magazine.

Today, Annella offers a diverse range of programs and services, including performance improvement coaching, behavior-based organizational design consulting, customized workshops and seminars, and powerful keynote speeches. She is her clients' trusted advisor and assists her audiences in achieving major shifts.

To contact her, please visit her website, www.annellametoyer.com

Lightning Source UK Ltd.
Milton Keynes UK
UKHW020756110821
388656UK00002B/366